A HOTEL IS A PLACE...

By Shelley Berman

Designed and Illustrated by Ed Powers

PRICE / STERN / SLOAN
Publishers, Inc., Los Angeles

Other Books By Shelley Berman

Cleans & Dirtys

Copyright © 1972 by Shelley Berman
Illustrations Copyright © 1972 by Price/Stern/Sloan Publishers, Inc.
Published by Price/Stern/Sloan Publishers, Inc.
410 North La Cienega Boulevard, Los Angeles, California 90048
Printed in the United States of America. All rights reserved.
Library of Congress Catalog Card Number: 72-91529
ISBN: 0-8431-0211-X

TO
The RALJON folks,
GENTLEMAN JACK and LADY JEAN
JOHN and BECKY

and in the East
MIKE and MICHAEL

IF THEY RAN HOTELS I'D HAVE NOTHING TO WRITE ABOUT

TABLE OF CONTENTS

INTRODUCTION

or

About the Title

Not long ago I checked into a fashionable and long respected New York hotel.

When the desk clerk was convinced I had a reservation he handed me the usual registration card to fill out. The information requested was:

1. The date.
2. My name (PLEASE PRINT).
3. My home address.
4. My home phone number.
5. My city, state and zip code.
6. The name of my firm.
7. The firm's address.
8. The firm's phone number.
9. The firm's city, state and zip code.
10. My signature.

It was like applying for unemployment compensation.

The clerk read my filled-out card. He then called a bellman who took a key from the desk, grabbed my luggage and, in a crisp, businesslike voice, said: "Follow me sir." I followed.

I had no idea where we were going. My orders were to follow so, of course, I followed. Chased, actually. The speedy bellman was a whiz at negotiating elevators and corridors. And he had the added advantage of knowing where he was taking me. I, on the other hand, was not even sure he was leading me to a room. I hadn't even noticed what floor we were on.

All I knew was I had apparently passed my registration card exam with flying colors and was now proving myself a born follower.

Along the way a thought took shape in my mind: A hotel is a place where when you check in *they* ask all the questions and *you* give all the answers.

This gave way to more rebellious thoughts. Why did *I* have to do all the registering? After all, wasn't I paying for the room? Why hadn't I given the *desk clerk* a card to fill out?

1. Location, floor and room number of hotel room.
2. Number of windows and type of view.
3. TV set? If yes:
   (a) Color, or black and white.
   (b) Working, or needs a tube.
4. Number of drawers.
5. Volume of closet space (in cubic feet).
6. Location of bed, size of bed, brand name of mattress.
7. Name, address and home phone number of desk clerk (PLEASE PRINT).

⟫⟶

Later, in my room, I took my suitcase off the folding luggage rack and put it on the bed so I could unpack it. I had a new thought: A hotel is a place where your suitcase is always put on one of those stupid folding luggage racks on which it is absolutely impossible to unpack a suitcase.

That thought led to another: A hotel is a place with stupid folding luggage racks which, when unfolded, are useless and in the way and, when folded, can't stand up anyplace and you don't know what the hell to do with them. You can drive yourself crazy trying to lean a folded luggage rack on the closet wall because they are especially designed to slide down and fall on the floor.

Anyway, this made me think of my closet. I went to it but the door was locked. It wasn't a closet at all. It was one of the basic locked doors which are always found in hotel rooms. I thought: A hotel is a place where your room always contains at least one mystery door which is locked to you and behind which there undoubtedly lurks some terrible secret.

More and more revelatory thoughts came to me — curious and bizarre conclusions about hotel-dwelling which till now I had always regarded as perfectly reasonable. The most stunning conclusion of all was that hotels are in fact sovereign territories. They have their own language, their own criteria for behavior, their own definitions for comfort and service.

Think about the last time you were in a posh hotel and you ordered room service. Remember the table being opened up and the waiter laying out the meal — the silver, the dishes, the splendid looking food? Remember his "Anything else, sir?" Remember you had three chairs in your room and *not a single one was tall enough for you to sit at that gorgeous table and eat properly?* Remember how that gorgeous table was chin-high when you sat to eat?

But did you complain? Of course not. You scrounged around for cushions. You did not regard it as lunacy. You simply accepted it as "hotelish."

Since hotels are "hotelish" — in fact, *alien* — how can an ordinary man describe a hotel in one sentence?

If he really thinks about it he'll say: "A hotel is a place . . . " And stop right there.

Shelley Berman
Beverly Hills, California

A HOTEL IS A PLACE where you get out of a taxi with two suitcases and an attaché case and the Doorman says, "Are you checking in, Sir?"

A HOTEL IS A PLACE...

Where You Almost Never

Get To Finish Saying,

"Who's There?"

or

Maids, Invasion Techniques of...

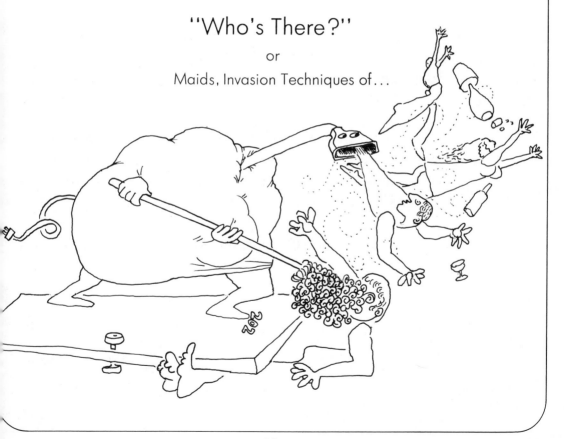

In most of the civilized world a knock-knock on the door means, "Is anyone home?"

In a hotel a knock-knock means, "Coming in, ready or not!" *

What really distinguishes the hotel knock-knock from your everyday knock-knock is that in the case of the hotel knock-knock the one who does the knock-knocking *is also the one who opens the door.*

In the everyday knock-knock the person *inside* first gets to say, "Who's there?" and, when satisfied that the one *outside* is not a homicidal maniac, he may then open the door *from the inside* and let the knock-knocker in.

In a hotel the door is almost always opened *from the outside.*

*Variations on the hotel knock-knock:
1. "Are you going to sleep all day, you lazy lout you?"
2. "Yes, I see your 'Do Not Disturb' sign, but you're my last room and it's four o'clock already and I can't go home until I find out if you want service or not and I'm just wondering if you're dead in there or something!"

Q. What else distinguishes the hotel knock-knock from the garden variety knock-knock?

A. In a hotel the knock-knock and the opening of the door are simultaneous.

Moreover, entry by the knock-knocker into your room is so immediate that — light and sound being what they are — you may actually find yourself confronted by your maid a good four-tenths of a second *prior* to hearing the knock-knock!

Q. Why is this?

A. It is because hotel maids have a highly developed sense of intrusion. (Not to be confused with sense of interruption, generally confined to restaurant waiters).

Q. How does it work?

A. Please see following sample occasions. ⋙→

"Knock-knock."
"Who's ————?"
"Oops. Sorry. I didn't know you were in."
(Note the unfinished "Who's there?")

"Knock-knock."
"???"
"Oops. Sorry. Just checking."
(Insufficient time to utter "Who's there?")

"Oops sorry, thought you were out." — (knock-knock)
"!!!"
(No time to even *think* "Who's there?" Knock-knock heard after maid's full sentence.)

Read the following conversation very carefully.

MAID: Oops. Sorry. Your 'Do Not Disturb' sign isn't on your door.

YOU: I shouted who's there. Didn't you hear me shout who's there?

MAID: Yes, but I was in already. Should I come back later?

YOU: Of course come back later. Come back later!

MAID: As long as I'm here, should I make the bed?

YOU: No, not now! Later!

MAID: You didn't put out your 'Do Not Disturb' sign.

YOU: For God's sake!

MAID: How about if I come back in a half hour?

YOU: Fine. Fine. Come back in a half hour.

MAID: All rightee. I'll be back in a half hour. ⟫→

How would you classify the preceding conversation?

    a. pleasant?
    b. unpleasant?
    c. unbearable?

The correct answer would be c. *unbearable.*

Q. Why?

A. You were naked.

A HOTEL IS A PLACE...

Where There Are Three Drawers And Yours Is
The Second From The Bottom

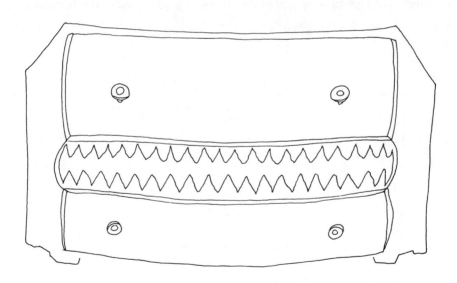

Once, during a night club routine, I made some snide re-marks about insufficient drawer space in hotels. A few days later I got a letter from a man who claimed he had been stay-ing in hotels for years and had always found ample drawer space. The letter writer turned out to be a midget who was allergic to socks and underwear.

Most of the newer hotel rooms are equipped with a combi-nation desk-dressing table. The desk portion contains one drawer and the dressing table portion has two.

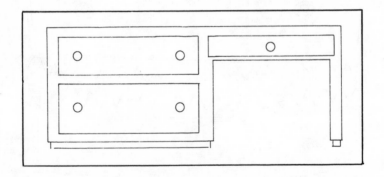

Q. Isn't this a total of three drawers?

A. No. This is an illusion of three drawers.

To understand the true nature of hotel drawer space, one must first have a comprehension of hotel drawer dimension and function.

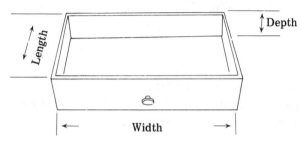

The desk drawer
    Depth: 4 handkerchiefs (folded twice; pressed well)
    Length: ¾ of an undershirt
    Width: 2 Manila envelopes plus 1 cufflink case

Top dresser drawer (or second from bottom)
    Depth: 3 shirts (laundry folded; all cardboard removed)
    Length: 1 stretch sock (knee length)
    Width: 3½ jockey shorts

Bottom dresser drawer (the largest)
    Depth: 2 golf shirts plus 1 alpaca cardigan
    Length: 1 pajama bottom (folded once)
    Width: 1 legal pad, 1 stack expense receipts and
             1 pajama top

⋙→

Reading the dimensions you may get the idea there is plenty of drawer space. Not really.

The desk drawer is there for your convenience, not your socks. It contains:

(1) A folder of hotel stationery.
(2) Picture postcards with a fantastically gorgeous picture of a hotel that has the same name as yours.
(3) A telegram pad.
(4) Two 'no disturb' signs.
(5) A room service menu.
(6) A dry ballpoint pen.
(7) A Gideon Bible.

Most of this stuff you could remove and put on the dresser top, if you had room on the dresser top. But your dresser top is usually crowded with the things you couldn't put in the bathroom because there are no shelves and the medicine cabinet was filled with three wrapped glasses, three little bars of soap, two wrapped face cloths, an extra roll of toilet paper and a courtesy shoe-cloth.

Besides, I don't know about you but I feel a little funny about displacing the Bible for three pairs of undershorts.

So you are left with one drawer — the top drawer of the dresser.

Q. Why can't you use the bottom drawers?

A. Because that's where they keep the extra blanket, dummy.

A HOTEL IS A PLACE
where if you don't have an
identification badge
that tells your name and
the name of your company
you feel left out.

A HOTEL IS A PLACE...

With A Staff

THE DESK CLERK

RING BELL.

The DESK CLERK'S job is very hard.

He is in charge of your keys, messages and mail. He greets you. He is the first person you deal with when you enter the hotel to check in. His primary mission, however, is to inform you that you do not have a reservation. ⇒→

When you say, "I *do* have a reservation!" the DESK CLERK smiles pleasantly at your bald-faced lie. Whenever a problem such as this arises the DESK CLERK invariably says, "Obviously there's been some kind of misunderstanding." Then he smiles at you.

Q. What does it mean when the DESK CLERK says, "Obviously there's been some kind of misunderstanding," and smiles at you?

A. It means as far as the DESK CLERK is concerned everything is all cleared up and you now have his permission to go away.

In most cases you will find the DESK CLERK'S solution unacceptable and you will decline his permission to go away. There are two courses of action open to you:

1. Ask to speak to the manager.
2. Sing "We Shall Overcome."

The DESK CLERK is always ready for the "manager bit." He will answer, "I'm sorry but the manager is out to lunch and won't be back for forty-five minutes."

If you should respond, "But it's seven o'clock in the morning!" the DESK CLERK will look up at you with what appears to be tears in his eyes and say , "I'm really awfully sorry."

Q. What does it mean when the DESK CLERK looks up at you with tears in his eyes and says, "I'm really awfully sorry"?

A. Nothing.

In the event you persist in demanding accommodations, claiming you do have a reservation, the DESK CLERK will say, "I can't tell you how bad I feel about this."

It's seven in the morning, you have a business meeting scheduled for 9 a.m., your plane was an hour late leaving L.A., you missed a connection in Chicago and waited two hours at the airport for another plane, one of your bags is en route to Tulsa, Oklahoma, you're trying to check into a hotel that doesn't have a record of your reservation and the DESK CLERK is telling you how bad *he* feels. ⇛→

Q. Does the DESK CLERK really feel bad?

A. Not nearly as bad as he's going to feel if he looks up and smiles just one more goddam time!

THE BELLMAN

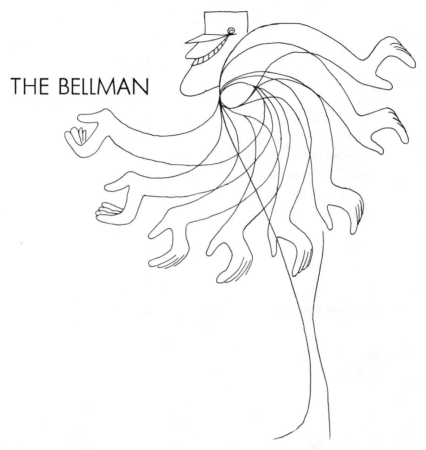

The BELLMAN is a very helpful person. It was impossible to write about him in detail because every time I said the word "BELLMAN" my hand would involuntarily leap from the typewriter and reach into my pocket for change.

A HOTEL IS A PLACE
where you can be in
your room from 3 p.m. to 3:30 p.m.
and then go to the desk and
pick up a phone message
which came in at 3:15 p.m.

THE OPERATOR

The OPERATOR is your only link with the outside world.

You need her desperately. She knows this. She is very helpful.

For example, if you leave a "wake-up" call for 7 a.m., the next morning your phone will ring and she will say, "Good morning, it's ten after seven." She says this pleasantly.

Sometimes the OPERATOR will scare you. If you are staying at the BRINEY-HIVERLY HOTEL and dial the OPERATOR she will answer, "Briney-Hiverly. Good morning."

Q. Why does it scare you when the OPERATOR says, "Briney-Hiverly. Good morning."?

A. Because that answer makes you feel as if you are calling from outside the BRINEY-HIVERLY.

Sometimes the OPERATOR makes you wait a very long time before she responds to your call. Why? Check the reason you think is correct.

1. She is busy.
2. She is asleep.
3. She has left her post.
4. She hates you.

The correct answer is all of the above. She was so busy hating you she wandered away from her post and went to sleep.

Would you like to play a dirty trick on the OPERATOR? Here's what to do next time the OPERATOR takes a century before responding.

When she finally does answer, you say, "It's all right now. I was able to put the fire out by myself." Then hang up quickly.

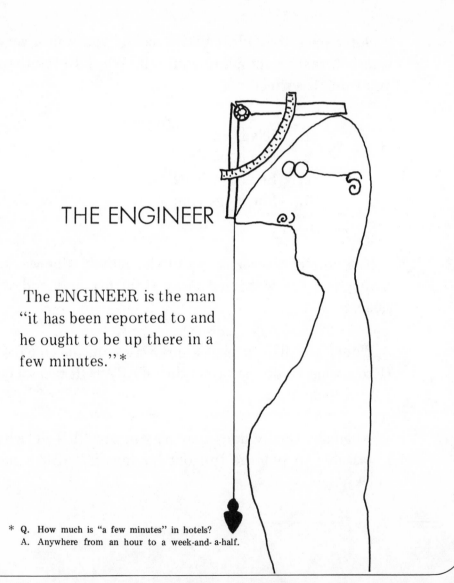

THE ENGINEER

The ENGINEER is the man "it has been reported to and he ought to be up there in a few minutes."*

* Q. How much is "a few minutes" in hotels?
  A. Anywhere from an hour to a week-and- a-half.

The ENGINEER in a hotel is a man wise in the ways of things mechanical. He is never intentionally offensive. He cannot help it if you gain the mistaken impression that he thinks you are a dummy. So when you say to him, "My heater isn't working," and he asks, "Did you turn the knob to the 'on' position?" don't get upset. All he wants to know is if you know how to put your fingers on a knob and turn it and if you can read the word "on."

Actually you rarely get to talk to the ENGINEER by phone. It works like this. You dial the operator and say, "May I speak to the engineer, please?"

After a few minutes the operator says, "I'm sorry. I've been ringing but he doesn't pick up. He's probably busy. If you'll tell me what's wrong I'll report it to him and he'll take care of it in a few minutes."

"Well," you say, "the plug on my television set is broken. I mean the prongs are loose and I can't plug it in." ⟫→

"I'll report it to the ENGINEER," says the operator. "I'll tell him your TV set isn't working."

"Just the plug. If you'll just tell him the plug is broken."

"Sir. I said I'd report it. There's nothing more I can do."

"Thank you. All I need is a plug."

Q. What will the operator report to the ENGINEER?
A. "Room 1201. TV set."

When the ENGINEER does arrive you're in the shower, of course. ENGINEERS make it a point to arrive only when you're not in the room, when you're in the shower, when you're on long-distance or when your room service supper is being delivered.

Hotel ENGINEERS are like doctors. They always say, "What seems to be the trouble?" and then don't listen to your answer.

As you're saying, "The NBA playoffs began at six," he's looking at your TV set. The ENGINEER, with his vast knowledge, then proceeds to tell you what's wrong.

"It's not on," he says, "This set isn't turned on."

"I know," you answer.

"See this little knob that says 'on-off'? You have to press it in."

"I pressed it in," you plead. "I have one at home."

"Look," says the ENGINEER, "It's not plugged in. You see, sir, these sets have to be plugged in. They run on electricity."

⋙→

"I know that! I know! Didn't the operator tell you . . . ?"

"Here's your trouble right here," he says, "The plug's broken. You got a broken plug here."

"That's what I told her. I swear. I said the plug's broken!" You're fighting for the ENGINEER'S respect. For some idiotic reason you want this man to love you.

"No wonder this set won't work," the ENGINEER says. "Look at this right here. See? The prongs are loose."

"Loose prongs, eh?" you reply, having decided the hell with it.

"All you need is a new plug. Nothing's wrong with the set itself."

"Really? All I need is a new plug? Well I'll be darned," you say. It's a case of being resigned to the fact that the ENGINEER is convinced you are a dummy, but at least you want him to find you an *agreeable* dummy.

"Trouble is," the ENGINEER goes on, "the supply room is closed. I'll get a plug up here first thing in the morning."

CONCLUSION: When the ENGINEER arrives, stay in the shower.

Unless there's something wrong with the shower.

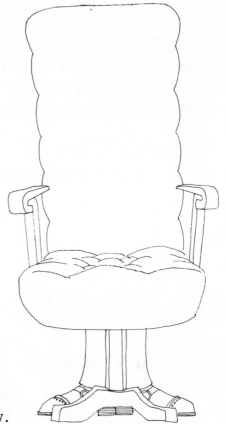

THE MANAGER

He's out of his office right now.
He's in a meeting.
He's not in yet.
He's out to lunch.
Do not hesitate to call if he can be of any assistance. Or contact the Assistant Manager.

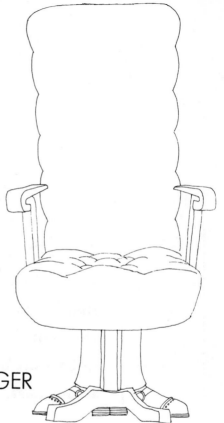

THE ASSISTANT MANAGER

He's out of his office right now.
He's in a meeting.
He's expected momentarily.
He's out to lunch.
Do not hesitate to call him if he can be of any assistance.

**A HOTEL
IS A PLACE**
that keeps
the manufacturers
of 25-watt bulbs
in business.

A HOTEL IS A PLACE
where the minute your
shower temperature is adjusted
somebody signals the
guy next door to flush his toilet
and scald you to death.

A HOTEL IS A PLACE
where "the double room
you reserved is not available
right now but we have a
nice single you can stay in tonight
and we'll move you
into the double
tomorrow afternoon."

A HOTEL IS A PLACE...
Where The Hangers Have No Hooks

The clothes-hanger in a hotel has a little T-shaped head where its hook should be.

The T-shaped head slips snugly into the notch at the bottom of the ring which is permanently fitted to the cross-bar which is fixed to the closet walls at either end so as to be unremovable.

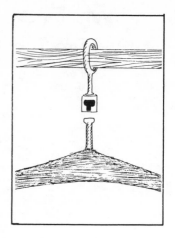

More simply:

The closet walls connected to the cross-bar -
the cross-bar connected to the hanger-ring -
the hanger-ring connected to the little notch -
the little notch connected to the hanger-head -
the hanger-head connected to the hanger -
the hanger connected to the suitcoat -
etc.

A mere glance at a hotel-type hanger and you know you are dealing with a device that may not be approached with anything less than two hands. Why am I pussyfooting? If you don't have three hands you can't use these goddam hangers.

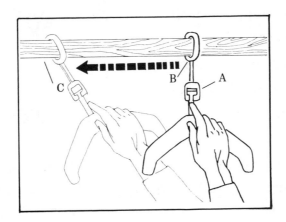

As hanger is raised vertically to disengage hanger-head from notch (A), hanger-ring (B) slides along cross-bar (C) on a horizontal plane (see arrow).

>>>→

You don't have to be an Einstein to figure out that one hand will have to steady the hanger-ring to keep it from sliding while the other hand is extricating the hanger. The question is which hand is holding the suit you want to hang? See illustration for what the hotel expects of you.

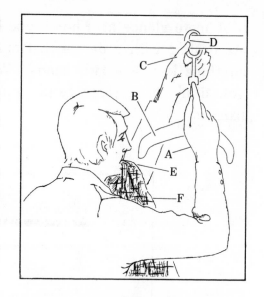

Right hand (A) extricates hanger (B) as left hand (C) steadies hanger-ring (D). Pay particular attention to mouth (E) which, since you don't have three hands, is holding suit (F).

WARNING: PROLONGED AND REPEATED USE OF THIS PROCEDURE MAY RESULT IN PERMANENT TOOTH-MARKS IN YOUR LAPELS.

Q. Is a hotel the only place where you can find hangers without hooks?

A. No. You can also find them in a hookless hanger factory.

Q. Did somebody actually invent the hookless hanger?

A. Yes. A person actually spent many years developing a way to make hanging clothes harder. We are not at liberty to divulge his name but you'll know him the minute you see him. His lapels are covered with tooth-marks.

Q. Did the inventor of the hookless hanger invent anything else?

A. We don't know for sure. There is some talk that he holds a patent on an automobile door that opens inwards.

Q. Why do hotels use hangers without hooks?

A. Because hotel guests often inadvertently pack regular hangers in their suitcases. There is no sense in inadvertently packing a hanger without a hook.

**A HOTEL
IS A PLACE**
where the room
service waiter
puts a perfectly
rare steak in
a warmer so it can
be nice and well-done
when it gets
to your room.

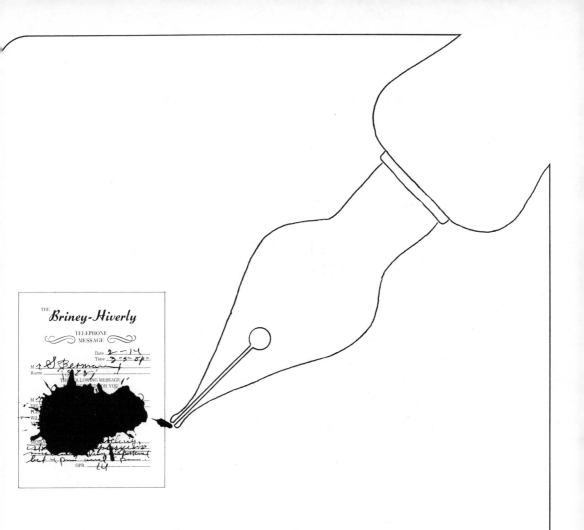

A HOTEL IS A PLACE...

Where A Telephone Message Is A Telephone Message Is A Telephone Message...

This chapter is so complex it will be necessary to divide it into two parts.

I.   HOTEL TELEPHONE MESSAGE FORM — THE OVERPRINT PRINCIPLE.

II. HOW TO READ THE OPERATOR'S HANDWRITING AND WHAT TO DO WHEN YOU FAIL.

PART I.   HOTEL TELEPHONE MESSAGE FORM — THE OVERPRINT PRINCIPLE

1.   It's your day off and you've gone to the hardware store for a screwdriver. You get home and your wife says, "Joe called. He's got the flu and can't play handball tomorrow."

2.   You come back into the office after having gone out for a screwdriver. Your secretary says, "Joe Smith called. He's at 555-2368."

Hotels feel telephone messages such as the above are unworthy of you.

You think all you want to know is: Who Called — What He Said — Where He Can Be Reached. Hotels give you more — much more — than these bland colorless bits of vital information.

Turn the page for a look at a typical hotel telephone message and see THE OVERPRINT PRINCIPLE in action.

⟫→

THE

Briney-Hiverly

TELEPHONE
MESSAGE

Date _____

Time _____ m

M _____

Room _____

THE FOLLOWING MESSAGE
WAS RECEIVED FOR YOU
from

M _____

TEL. NO. _____

PLEASE RETURN CALL ☐

WILL CALL AGAIN ☐

YOUR LINE WAS BUSY ☐

MESSAGE _____

_____

_____

_____

OPR. _____

This form contains 20 individual informational lines or spaces. It is made up of:

27 printed whole words
6 printed abbreviations
11 printed straight lines
3 printed little boxes
2 printed pairs of curlicues

This is a grand total of **49** special printed ingredients. Since many hotels give you an "original" down at the desk and a carbon copy under your door the total may be doubled. In other words, a hotel telephone message uses *40* spaces and lines containing *98* special printed ingredients just so you can know: Who Called — What He Said — Where He Can Be Reached.

Q. Why is this?

A. Because of THE OVERPRINT PRINCIPLE.

Q. What is the function of THE OVERPRINT PRINCIPLE?

A. It makes your telephone message an event! It is form and beauty!

THE OVERPRINT PRINCIPLE captures the imagination, makes your message a memorable experience! It is perfection! In the end THE OVERPRINT PRINCIPLE stands right up and says something important!

Q. What important thing does THE OVERPRINT PRINCIPLE stand right up and say?

A. "SCREW INFORMATION!"

The SIS or SCREW INFORMATION SYNDROME is an important by-product of THE OVERPRINT PRINCIPLE. Consider the following.

Q. When you're through with a hotel telephone message what do you do with it?

A. You save it. When you get home you find used hotel telephone messages in your luggage.

Q. Why do you save used hotel telephone messages?

A. You are afraid to throw them away. You are sure you'll want to study them again in the future. One of the symptoms of SIS is losing your faith in your own address book.

The final result of THE OVERPRINT PRINCIPLE is your ultimate conviction that:

♥ A TELEPHONE MESSAGE IS FOREVER.♥

Now for a closer look at THE OVERPRINT PRINCIPLE at work.   ⋙→

THE
Briney-Hiverly • ————————— 1

TELEPHONE •————————— 2
MESSAGE ————————— 3

Date _____ •————— 4
Time _____ m•————— 5

M _____ •————— 6
Room _____ •————— 7

THE FOLLOWING MESSAGE •————— 8
WAS RECEIVED FOR YOU •————— 9
from •————————————— 10

M _____ •————— 11
TEL. NO. _____ •————— 12
PLEASE RETURN CALL ☐ •————— 13
WILL CALL AGAIN ☐ •————— 14
YOUR LINE WAS BUSY ☐ •————— 15

MESSAGE _____ •————— 16
_____ •————— 17
_____ •————— 18
_____ •————— 19
OPR. _____ •————— 20

Let us assume you are a guest at the BRINEY-HIVERLY HOTEL and have just been handed this message. Let us assume you are the type who reads hotel telephone messages in the order in which they are presented — from top to bottom.

Q. Why would any normal person assume this form should be read from top to bottom?

A. Who said anything about normal? It's obvious the people who invented hotel telephone message forms said, "Let's assume all people who stay in hotels are complete idiots."

Now, read line 1. Write the information you obtain from line 1 on the lines below.

e.g.   1. *The name of the hotel I'm staying at.*

Read lines 2 and 3. What have you learned? Write on the line provided.

2. _____

3. _____

>>>→

Do the same with lines 4, 5, 6, 7, 8, 9 and 10.

4. _____
5. _____
6. _____
7. _____
8. _____
9. _____
10. _____

You have now read half your telephone message. What do you know now that you didn't know before? If your answer is the time the message was received (line 5) you are correct.

Q. What don't you know?

A. Who Called, What He Said and Where He Can Be Reached!

CONCLUSIONS:

1. Half of a hotel telephone message does not contain a telephone message.
2. About the only thing missing from a hotel telephone message is a Table of Contents.

THE TELEPHONE MESSAGE , PART II.

HOW TO READ THE OPERATOR'S HANDWRITING AND WHAT TO DO WHEN YOU FAIL

You have just received this hotel telephone message.

Let us first examine the caller's name.

Note that the operator has given you a multiple choice last name. Is it:

Danielson?
Davidson?
Darielson?

Note that in all cases the third letter of the last name is dotted, but in no case is that letter an *i*. It is not unusual for experienced hotel operators to dot n's, v's and r's. They are also in the habit of crossing l's, h's and any other vertical letter, including — but not always — t's. In fact a dot or a cross may merely indicate the presence of an *i* or a *t* in the message but have nothing to do with its actual location.

Hotel operators' crossing of t's may as well be studied at this point since the letter *t* in the hands of an operator is in great jeopardy. The cross of the *t* by the *same operator* in the *same message* may vary drastically from *t* to *t*.

Return to Town

pre-cross   after-cross   high-cross
(return)   (to)   (town)

take late wait

right-cross   left-cross   double-cross
(take)   (late)   (wait − note dotted *a*)

state

Is this word state? slate? or stale? This sample of *grand-cross* must appear in a sentence before it can be understood. There is a catch however. What if the rest of the sentence is filled with t's? Don't think about that.

⇛→

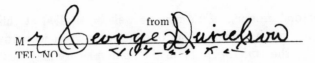

M ___ from ___
TEL. NO ___

Once you know the true spirit of a hotel operator's dots and crosses, you start suspecting other letters. Is the second letter of the last name an *a* or a *u?* Is that *l* which looks like an *f* actually an uncrossed *t?*

Dunietson?

Perhaps the fifth letter is not an *e* but an undotted *i* with a little loop in it.

Dursifron?
Dansitron?
Deiviekon?

Are you sure the last letter is an *n?* It might be a *u* or a *w.* Maybe it's two undotted *i*'s or two short uncrossed *t*'s.

Duriefrou?
Duimepsow?
Dumsitrott?

Look again at the second letter of the last name. If it's a *u* you're in luck. U's are famous for following q's around — all over the world except Iraq. (Iraq is therefore uniq). So the first letter might be a Q rather than a D.

Quimefsow?
Quimelrou?
Quirsefron?

Perhaps there is a hint in the first name. It is George. But *is* it George? Look at it again. According to the operator who took the message it begins with a treble clef.

Nobody named George spells his name with a treble clef. That treble clef could be a fancy S. And the fourth letter could be a *v*. The fifth letter might be a *y* rather than the more obvious *g.* This add up to the name, Seovye.

Q. Would anybody's first name be Seovye?

A. If his last name is Quirsefron there is no reason his first name shouldn't be Seovye.

Confirmation of the caller's identity may be found in the telephone number.

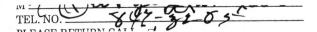

It is 847-3205. Or 847-32<u>65</u>. All you have to do is call 847-3205 and when a voice answers just say, "Hello, is Seovye Quirsefron or George Dumsitrott there?" When that person hangs up merely dial 847-3265 and try again. Having failed that you may as well go on to the next step — the message.

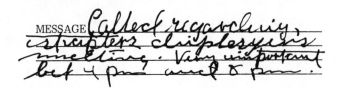

In reading the message pay particular attention to the first two words, "Called regarding." Despite the dotted g these are the only two words in the entire message which do not require special scrutiny. The rest of the message is a whole new story. What did Seovye Quirsefron or George Dumsitrott call regarding?

Does it say:

"ispaplers clirpleryers melting?"

If you are in the business of melting ispaplers clirpleryers (or *stopping* ispaplers clirpleryers from melting), the message is clear. If not, other possibilities are:

"strapless bricklayers meeting"
"stapler displayers smelling"

The rest of the message is, of course, quite clear: "Very important between 4 p.m. and 6 p.m." Or: "Very unimportant between 4 p.m. and 0 p.m.

Now that you have failed everything you must seek the assistance of the operator who took the message. So look at the operator's identification.

OPR.

OPR. _LL_

Pick up the phone and dial "Operator." Our studies have shown that what you will say to the voice that answers will come out very much like the following.

"Hello, may I speak to Operator L.U.? . . . That's funny, it looked like an L.U. Maybe it's a 24 or a 14. Got an Operator 24 or 14? . . . Well then, how about an Operator 2U or L4? . . . I see. Say you wouldn't have an Operator W down there, would you? . . . Any chance of a Roman numeral three? . . . Would you have a girl down there who recently emigrated from the Orient?"

Just sit back and relax. At least you can be sure the party will call again.

M
TEL. NO. _8 07 - 3 2 0 5_
PLEASE RETURN CALL ☐
WILL CALL AGAIN ☑
YOUR LINE WAS BUSY ☐

Or maybe he wants you to call him.

A HOTEL IS A PLACE where you can spend an evening looking for a lamp switch.

**A HOTEL
IS A PLACE**
where you're paying
about thirty bucks
a day and they're
calling you "guest."

A HOTEL IS A PLACE...

Where Leonard Bernstein

Should Have Such

Acoustics

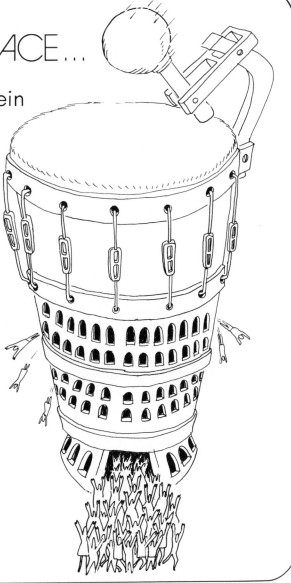

Q. What is it that hotels have every day except Saturday and Sunday from 8 a.m. to 5 p.m.?

A. Hammering.

Hammering is as much a part of a hotel as the building itself. If you find yourself in a hotel where there is no hammering you may as well check out as soon as possible because it is obvious this hotel does not pay attention to detail.

Q. What if the hotel is hammering on the ground floor and you are staying on the twelfth floor so you don't hear it?

A. The hotel is acoustically unsound. Get out.

Good hotels are constructed in a way that makes it possible for you to hear hammering from any point in the building.

It should be pointed out that the hammering is not always consistent. There are periods of no hammering which might make you anxious, but these periods are infrequent and short. Don't just up and leave a hotel the minute you don't hear hammering. Be patient and wait a bit. You'll soon hear hammering.

There is good hammering and bad hammering in hotels. The better hotels can be relied upon for good hammering.

Good hammering has two soft beats and five loud beats. The first two beats are short and quick, followed immediately by the five beats which have a distinct increase in tempo and volume. Each seven beat series sounds exactly alike in terms of tempo and volume. The pauses, however, are never predictable. You never know when the next nail is ready to be driven. Sometimes you actually think the last nail is in and suddenly the hammering starts again as you're in the middle of saying: "Thank God."

Bad hammering has a very consistent tempo and volume and seems to be coming from some specific place. You can never tell exactly where good hammering is coming from — you just know it's there.   ⇒→

Q. What is always next door to a hotel on the side of the building where your room is located?

A. Construction work.

Q. If your room is not on the side of the building where the construction work is taking place, should you be upset?

A. No. You'll hear it anyway.

The problem with construction work next door to a hotel is it makes it difficult for you to hear the hammering inside the hotel. But think of the guy whose room is next to the service elevator. He can't even hear the construction work. Heck, that poor guy can hardly hear the maids yelling to each other in the corridor.

Q. What if you want to take a nap?

A. There are no atheists in hotel rooms.

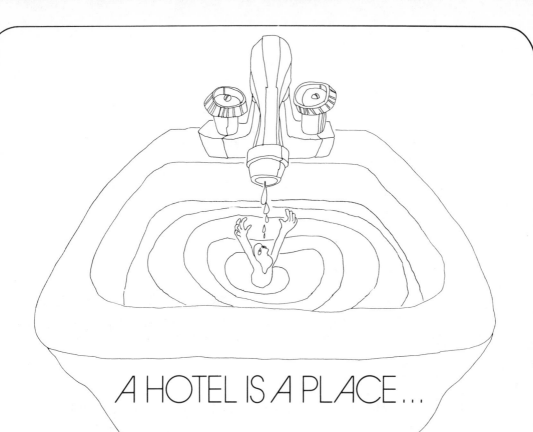

A HOTEL IS A PLACE...

Where You Can Find Diversion,
Mystery And Suspense,
or
COMING TO TERMS WITH YOUR
HOTEL BATHROOM

I. THE HOTEL SHOWER

Q. What do you need right after taking a shower in a hotel?

A. You need:
1. A bath towel.
2. A pair of galoshes.

Q. Why is this?

A. Because no matter how careful you are with the shower curtain, no matter how good you are at aiming the spray, a hotel shower will find a way to get an inch of water all over the bathroom floor.

There is nothing you can do about this so don't feel guilty about it. You are not a slob. You do not have to grab towels and mop up the floor. Just put on your galoshes and forget about it.

Hotels have several methods for flooding your bathroom floor but their favorite is the "WS," or, *WAYWARD SHPRITZER.*

Examine the following illustrations.

ORDINARY SHOWER

HOTEL SHOWER:
(Note Wayward Shpritzer)

The stream of water sent out by the WAYWARD SHPRITZER is called a "shpritz" (plural: shpritzi). Hotel shower shpritzi would be totally ineffective without a proper trajectory. The trajectory of a hotel shower shpritz is known as a "PITA." *

*PITA: the first two letters stand for Pain In ... Practically everything in a hotel is a PITA.

Let us follow a typical shpritz.

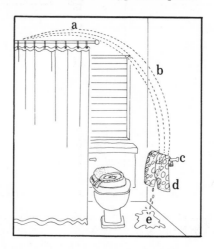

The shpritz (a); in a perfectly aimed PITA (b)   hits towel rack (c)   where you have hung your shorts (d). Your shorts drip the water onto the floor and begin flood (e). Without even knowing it you have wet your shorts. If that ain't a PITA, what is?

Do not — repeat *DO NOT* — mess with hotel shower-head spray adjuster. You may activate latent **WAYWARD SHPRITZERS** and wind up with a bathroom full of shpritzi. You will not know it until it's too late. You will step out of the shower and drown.

II. THE HOTEL BATHROOM EXHAUST FAN

Q. What is a hotel bathroom exhaust fan?

A. An insult.

A hotel bathroom exhaust fan says quite simply, "Every time you come into this room it is assumed you will foul up the air. Since we believe you are the kind of person who doesn't give a damn, we have made it impossible for you to come in here without the exhaust fan going on. The exhaust fan and the light are on a single switch so we can clean the air in spite of you."

Q. What is the most distinctive feature about a hotel bathroom exhaust fan?

A. The noise.

Something you've probably never noticed about yourself is a very silly thing you do just because the exhaust fan is so loud. Watch for it next time it happens to you.

We all know a toilet is flushing by the very fact that we hear it.

That's all the proof we need.

We listen for the flush and walk away.

In a hotel bathroom you can not hear the flush because of the exhaust fan. So you automatically *stand there like an idiot and watch your stupid toilet flushing!* You see the whole thing through to the end! If somebody walked in right then and asked you what the hell you're looking at, you'd die of humiliation.

Remember this? You were in your hotel bathroom, shaving, while your buddy, Fred, was sitting in your room having a drink. The bathroom door was open. The exhaust fan was going full blast. Fred's voice started the whole thing.

You heard, "Woowoo woomum wumbum oomumbum."

"What?"

"Wumbum! Woomum woowoo mumoomum? Oomumbum."

"What?"

"OOMUM! WOOMOO WOOHOOBUM! WOOHOOM!"

You walked out of the bathroom and said, "Sorry, Fred. I can't hear a word you're saying on account of that damn exhaust fan in there. What were you saying?"

"Oh, I was just asking if you could hear me in there with that damn exhaust fan going," Fred answered.

III. THE MEDICINE CABINET AND OTHER
PRACTICAL JOKES

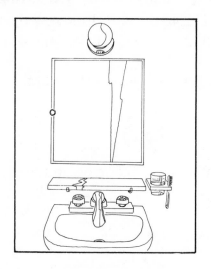

Q. What's wrong with this picture?

A. Everything.

Q. Why?

A. Because this is a hotel bathroom.

The shelf under the medicine cabinet is a Shelf On Brackets, or SOB. Let us put something on the SOB.

(Note Electric Shaver)

Now let us go ahead and use the medicine cabinet. Let's say you have a headache because of lack of oxygen which has been sucked out by the exhaust fan. Your aspirin is in the medicine cabinet.

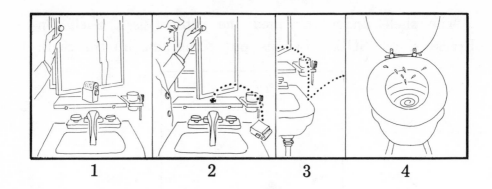

1   2   3   4

(1)   You innocently open cabinet door.

(2)   You do not realize SOB is placed too close to bottom of cabinet door. Bottom of cabinet door strikes electric shaver. Electric shaver is naturally knocked off of SOB.

(3)   In a perfect bank-shot, shaver caroms off washbasin.

(4)   Electric shaver falls into toilet. Of course.

In this instance part of the blame is your own. Anybody who has ever stayed in a hotel knows the importance of a closed toilet lid.

In a hotel bathroom a closed toilet lid is not only a necessity, it is a luxury.

A closed lid transforms a hotel toilet into:

(1) a chair.
(2) a safe and roomy shelf for your electric shaver and other tall items.
(3) a place to put your galoshes when taking a shower.
(4) a thing to stand on so you can look closely at the exhaust fan to see if there's a way to shut the damn thing off.
(5) a protective barrier for things which are knocked off the SOB every time you open the medicine cabinet.

A word of warning.

The closed toilet lid and the exhaust fan can conspire against you. Sometimes a person wakes in the middle of the night to use the bathroom. The person knows that the sound of the exhaust fan may wake him so completely he may not be able to fall back to sleep. So he may not turn on the bathroom light since that would mean the fan would also go on.

In the dark a closed toilet lid is not exactly a sleepy man's best friend.

⋙→

Now let us look inside the medicine cabinet.

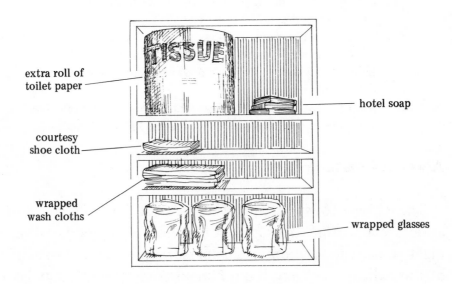

extra roll of
toilet paper

hotel soap

courtesy
shoe cloth

wrapped
wash cloths

wrapped glasses

This is it. The inside of your very own hotel bathroom cabinet. The hotel put it here especially for you to put all your toilet articles in. How handy and convenient!

So go ahead, put it all in — all those essentials you brought from home:

>toothbrush
>toothpaste (or denture cleanser)
>aerosol can of shaving cream
>razor (or rechargeable electric shaver)
>container of prescription medication
>bottle of aspirin
>dental floss

Don't just stand there looking, fella. Chuck the stuff in.

>aerosol can of deodorant
>nail clippers
>bottle of aftershave lotion
>box of foil-wrapped Alka Seltzer
>bottle or tube of hair dressing (or can of spray)
>vitamin E (doing you any good, fella?)
>comb
>hairbrush

Just go ahead and put it all away in this hotel bathroom cabinet. That's what it's there for, right? Right? Still wondering what a PITA is?

IV.

SANITIZED FOR YOUR PROTECTION

What does that strip of paper really mean? While your room was being readied for your occupancy did a man in a white smock and a face mask and rubber gloves remove the toilet seat, take it downstairs and boil it for fifteen minutes? When they replaced it did they hold it with forceps? Did they use a stainless steel, chromium plated, sterile screwdriver? That strip of paper costs money.

Somebody actually manufactures it, prints it. Somebody says, "We're running low on toilet seat strips. Better order some." They're counted, prepared, carried, painstakingly placed.

The whole idea is mind-boggling. Is the strip patented? Does the wording have a copyright? Who was the author?

All in all it's one hell of a big fuss just to let you know you've got a clean toilet seat. God knows, *somebody* must be taking it seriously.

But I can't. I really can't.

Want to have some fun and drive your maid out of her mind?

Carefully slide the strip off the seat and hide it. The next day, before leaving the room, carefully replace the strip. The more days you're staying at the hotel the more fun it gets to be. Just keep putting it back on before leaving the room. Pretty soon you'll notice that your maid runs and hides when she sees you walking down the corridor. If you can find her, walk up to her very casually and say, "I wonder if you could please do something about that strip on my toilet seat. It's really very inconvenient."

The look in her eyes will warm your heart!

A HOTEL IS A PLACE
where when you call
down to ask whatever happened
to your room service order
it's always
"on its way up right now,"
or "the waiter just left
the kitchen with it."

A HOTEL IS A PLACE...

Where The 14th Floor Is The 13th Floor In Disguise

Let us first learn how to read this typical elevator button panel in a large hotel.

L is for Lobby. The Lobby is on the first floor of the hotel.

LL is for Lower Lobby. Nobody knows why a hotel has a Lower Lobby, including the architect. The LL is just below the L which is the first floor. Think of it this way:

The LL is the first first floor.
The L is the second first floor.

So, if your elevator is going down, you arrive:

At the second first floor first.
At the first first floor second.

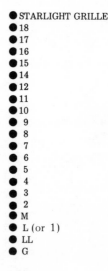

G does not mean Ground Floor. Many people make this mistake. They get out of the elevator and wonder why all those cars are parked in the Lobby. G is for Garage.

M is for Mezzanine. If you're riding down to the Lobby and the elevator happens to stop at the Mezzanine you will automatically get out and stand there wondering where the Lobby went. You can't help it. When you see you've passed floor number 2, your mind tells you that the next stop will be floor number 1.   But in hotels, between 2 and 1 is M.

Refer again to your button panel and look between 12 and 14.

Now you begin to see how that middle-class logic of yours goes over in hotels.

• Between 12 and 14 there is room for *something* but there is *nothing.*

• Between 1 and 2 there is room for *nothing* but there is *something.*

• A 19 story hotel is only 18 stories high.

• A Mezzanine is a floor which everybody gets out on but nobody counts.

If your conclusions don't terrify you, you're an idiot.

⟫→

Q. Why should your conclusions terrify you?

A. There is no 13th floor! You're in an elevator ten flights up. Your life is in the hands of people who are so convinced 13 is an unlucky number they left a whole damn floor out of their hotel!

Q. What is the truth about the 14th floor?

A. It is the 13th floor. If you accept a room on the 14th floor you're asking for trouble.

Q. Is it possible that the Mezzanine is really the second floor in disguise? If so, what is the truth about the 12th floor?

A. A HOTEL IS A PLACE with two 13th floors. A tall hotel is twice as unlucky as a short hotel.

A HOTEL IS A PLACE...

That Gives FREE Soap

Dear Maid,

Please do not leave any more of those little bars of soap in my bathroom since I have brought my own bath-size Dial. Please remove the six unopened little bars from the shelf under the medicine chest and another three in the shower soap dish. They are in my way. Thank you.

S. Berman

Dear Room 635,

I am not your regular maid she will be back tomorrow (Thurs) from her day off. I took the 3 hotel soaps out of the shower soap dish as you requested. The 6 bars on your shelf I took out of your way and put on top of your Kleenex dispenser in case you should change your mind. This leaves only the 3 bars I left today which my instructions from the management is to leave 3 soaps daily I hope this is satisfactory. If anything else comes up please call Mrs. Corum in the linen room.

Kathy (relief maid)

Dear Maid (I hope you are my regular maid),

Apparently Kathy did not tell you about my note to her concerning the little bars of soap. When I got back to my room this evening I found you had added 3 little Camays to the shelf under my medicine cabinet. I am going to be here in the hotel for two weeks and have brought my own bath-size Dial so I won't need those 6 little Camays which are now on the shelf. They are in my way when shaving, brushing teeth, etc. Please remove them.

S. Berman

Dear Mr. Berman,

My day off was last Wed so the relief maid left 3 hotel soaps which we are instructed by the management. I took the 6 soaps which were in your way on the shelf and put them in the soap dish where your Dial was. I put the Dial in the medicine cabinet for your convenience. I didn't remove the 3 complimentary soaps which are always placed inside the medicine cabinet for all new check-ins and which you did not object to when you checked in last Monday. Also I did place 3 hotel soaps on your shelf as per my instructions from the management since you left no instructions to the contrary. Please let me know if I can be of further assistance or call the linen room her name is Mrs. Korm. Have a pleasant stay.

Your regular maid, Dotty

Dear Mr. Berman,

The assistant manager, Mr. Kensedder, informed me this a.m. that you called him last evening and said you were unhappy with your maid service. I have assigned a new girl to your room. I hope you will accept my apologies for any past inconvenience. If you have any future complaints please contact me so I can give it my personal attention. Call extension 1108 between 8 a.m. and 5 p.m. Thank you.

Elaine Carmen, Housekeeper

Dear Miss Carmen,

It is impossible to contact you by phone since I leave the hotel for business at 7:45 a.m. and don't get back before 5:30 or 6 p.m. That's the reason I

⇥→

called Mr. Kensedder last night. You were already off duty. I only asked Mr. Kensedder if he could do anything about those little bars of soap. I did not want a new maid. The new maid you assigned me must have thought I was a new check-in today, since she left another 3 bars of hotel soap in my medicine cabinet along with her regular delivery of 3 bars on the bathroom shelf. In just five days here I have accumulated 24 little bars of soap. I'm beginning to dread the next 9 days. Why are you doing this to me?

S. Berman

Dear Mr. Berman,

Your maid Kathy, has been instructed to stop delivering soap to your room and remove the extra soaps. If I can be of further assistance, please call extension 1108 between 8 a.m. and 5 p.m. Thank you.

Elaine Carmen, Housekeeper

Dear Mr. Kensedder,

My bath-size Dial is missing. Every bar of soap was taken from my room including my own bath-size Dial. I came in late last night and had to call the bellhop to bring me a bar of soap so I could take a shower. He brought me 4 little Cashmere Bouquets.

S. Berman

Dear Mr. Berman,

I have informed our Housekeeper, Elaine Karmin, of your soap problem. I cannot understand why there was no soap in your room since our maids are instructed to leave three bars of soap each time they service a room. The situation will be rectified immediately. Please accept my apologies for the inconvenience. If you prefer Cashmere Bouquet to Camay, please contact Mrs. Karmin on extension 1108. Thank you.

Martin L. Kensedder
Assistant Manager

Dear Mrs. Carmen,

Who the hell left 54 little bars of Camay in my room? I came in last night and found 54 little bars of soap. I don't want 54 little bars of Camay. I want my 1 damn bar of bath-size Dial. Do you realize I have 58 bars of soap in here? All I want is my bath-size Dial. Give me back my bath-size Dial.

S. Berman

Dear Mr. Berman,

You complained of too much soap in your room so I had them removed. Then you complained to Mr. Kensedder that all your soap was missing so I personally returned them; the 24 Camays which had been taken and the 3 Camays you are supposed to receive daily. I don't know anything about the 4 Cashmere Bouquets. Obviously your maid Kathy did not know I had returned your soaps so she also brought 24 Camays plus the 3 daily Camays. I don't know where you got the idea that this hotel issues bath-size Dial. I was able to locate some hotel-size bath-size Ivory which I left in your room. We are doing our best here to satisfy you.

Elaine Carmen, Housekeeper

Dear Mrs. Carmen,

Just a short note to bring you up-to-date on my latest soap inventory. As of today I possess:

On shelf under medicine cabinet: 18 Camay in 4 stacks of 4 and 1 stack of 2.
On Kleenex dispenser: 11 Camay in 2 stacks of 4 and 1 stack of 3.
On bedroom dresser: 1 stack of 3 Cashmere Bouquet, 1 stack of 4 hotel-size bath-size Ivory, 8 Camay in 2 stacks of 4.
Inside medicine cabinet: 14 Camay in 3 stacks of 4 and 1 stack of 2.
In shower soap dish: 6 Camay (very moist).
On northeast corner of tub: 1 Cashmere Bouquet (slightly used).
On northwest corner of tub: 6 Camay in 2 stacks of 3.

Please ask Kathy when she services my room to make sure the stacks are neatly piled and dusted. Also, please advise her that stacks of more than 4 have a tendency to tip. May I suggest that my bedroom window sill is not in use and will make an excellent spot for future soap deliveries. One more item. I have purchased another bar of bath-size Dial which I am keeping in the hotel vault in order to avoid future misunderstandings.

S. Berman

A HOTEL
IS A PLACE
where you can
keep in condition
by leaping the
trays of dirty dishes
in the corridor.

A HOTEL IS A PLACE...
Where You Have Strange Conversations
or
Room Service

Reading hints: You are on the phone. The other party is also in the hotel.

Morny, rune sore-bees.

Oh sorry, I thought I dialed room service.

Rye. Rune sore-bees. Morny. Jewish to odor sunteen?

Yes, order something. This is room thirteen- oh-five. I want . . .

Okay, torino-fie. Yes plea?

I'd like some bacon and eggs.

Ow July then?

What?

Aches. Ow July then? Pry, boy, pooch . . . ?

Oh, the eggs! How do I like them! Sorry. Scrambled, please.

Ow July thee baycome? Crease?

Crisp will be fine.

Okay. An Santos?

What?

Santos. July Santos?

Uh . . . I don't know . . . I don't think so.

No? Judo one toes?

Look, I really feel bad about this, but I just don't know what judo-one-toes means. I'm sorry . . .

Toes! Toes! Why Jew Don Juan toes? Ow bow eenlish mopping we bother?

English muffin! I've got it! Toast! You were saying toast! Fine. An English muffin will be fine.

We bother?

No. Just put the bother on the side.

Wad?

I'm sorry. I meant butter. Butter on the side.

Copy?

I feel terrible about this but . . .

Copy. Copy, tea, mill . . .

Coffee!! Yes, coffee please. And that's all.

One Minnie. Ass rune torino-fie, strangle-aches, crease baycome, tossy eenlish mopping we bother honey sigh, and copy. Rye?

Whatever you say.

Okay. Tenjewberrymud.

You're welcome.

A HOTEL IS A PLACE where you come out of the entrance with two suitcases and an attaché case and the Doorman says, "Leaving us, Sir?"

ABOUT THE AUTHOR

Shelley Berman, one of our most brilliant comedy writers and performers, is equally at home in motion pictures, supper clubs, television and the legitimate theater.

An actor as well as a comedian, he has appeared in many stage roles and in dramatic parts on major TV shows. He most recently played the leading role in a touring company of *Fiddler on the Roof* and starred in the national touring company of *Two by Two*, which enabled him to stay in a great many hotels and do the definitive research on this book.

This multi-talented performer has always written his own material, as well as material for other performers and numerous variety and situation comedy shows for television. He is also author of the book *Cleans & Dirtys*, a hilarious treatise on the vagaries of language.

The Bermans (Sarah, Shelley, and their two children, Joshua and Rachel) live in Beverly Hills with their five French poodles.